W9-BUE-086

DINOSAURS ACROSS AMERICA

PHIL YEH

NANTIER · BEALL · MINOUSTCHINE
Publishing inc.
new york

Phil Yeh began publishing in 1970 at the age of 16 and has since written and illustrated more than 87 books, comics and graphic novels. In addition, Yeh founded Cartoonists Across America & The World in 1985 to promote literacy, creativity, and the arts through mural painting events, school and library workshops on comics and his series of non-violent and humorous books. Yeh's band of artists have painted more than 1600 colorful murals promoting literacy in more than 14 countries. He has been a guest artist at book festivals worldwide including the 1995 Bologna International Children's Book Fair, the 1995 Beijing Children's Book Fair, the 2002 Frankfurt Bookfair and many others. Yeh's work has been featured on a postage stamp in Hungary and he has been honored at the White House by former First Lady Barbara Bush.

ISBN 10: 1-56163-509-X
ISBN 13: 978-1-56163-509-2
© 2007 Phil Yeh
Colors by Lieve Jerger
Printed in China
5 4 3 2 1

4

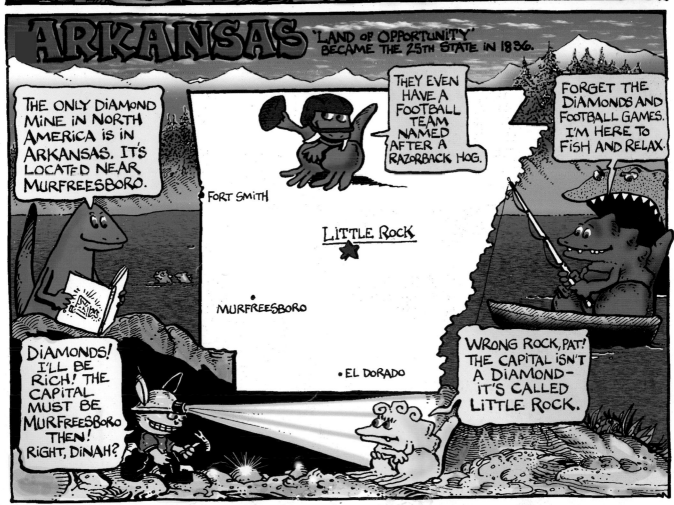

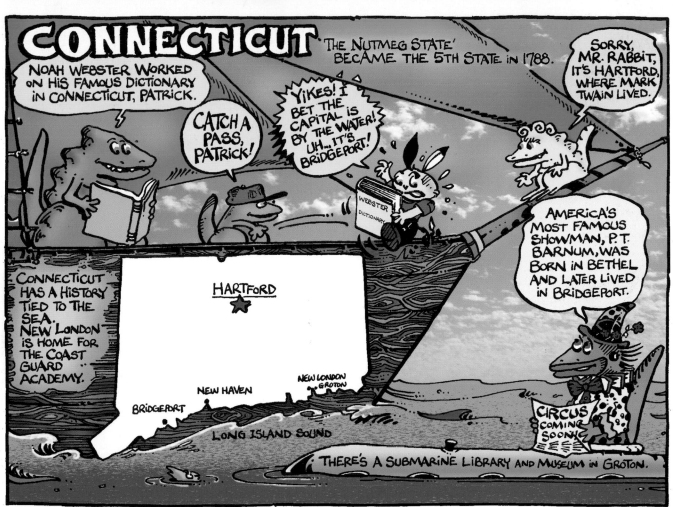

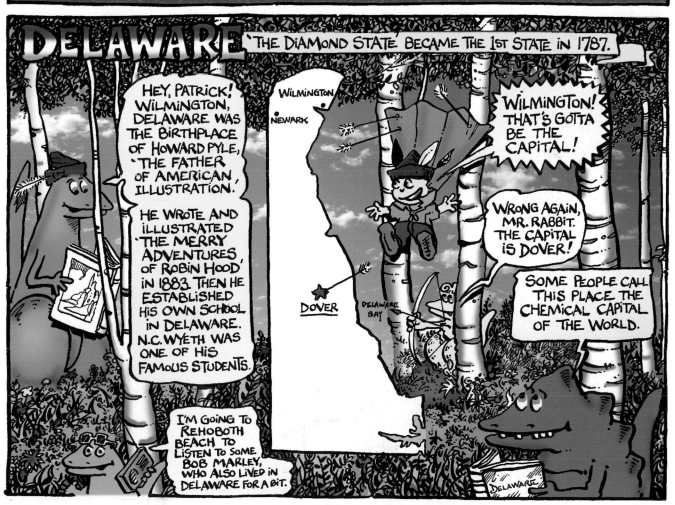

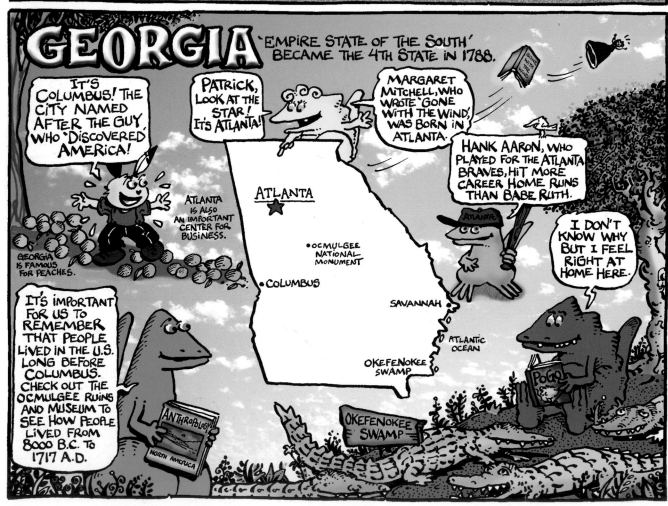

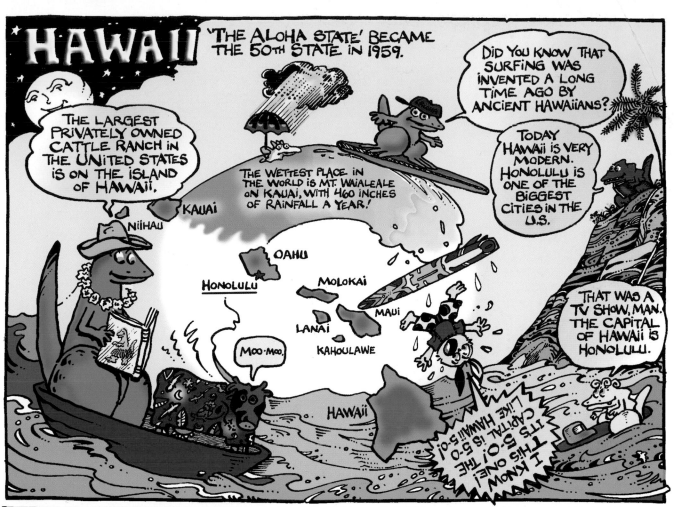

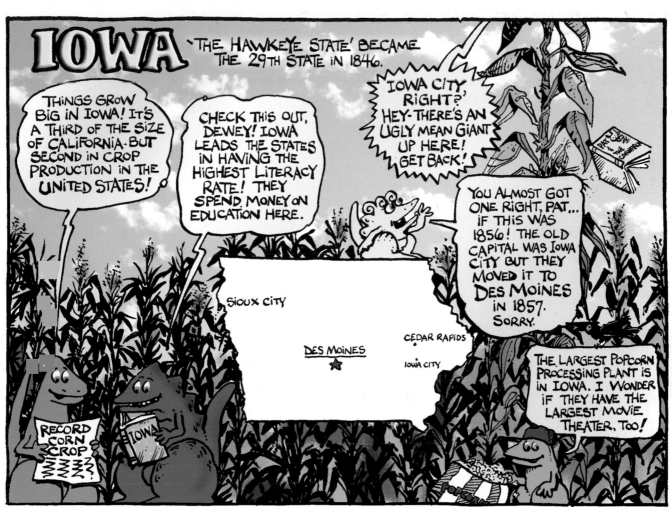

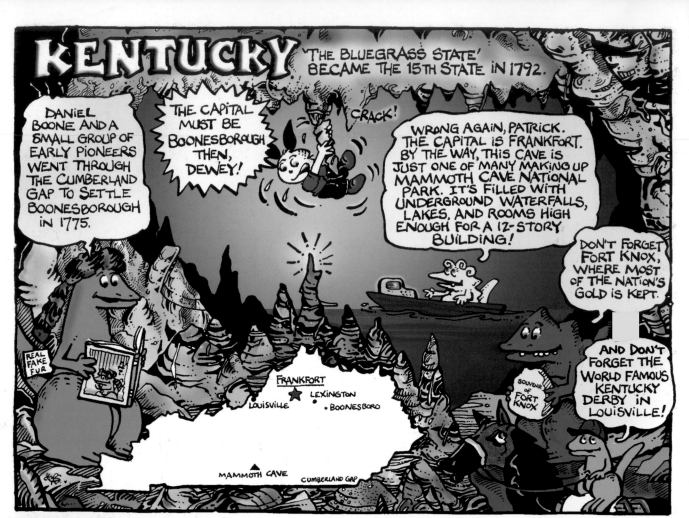

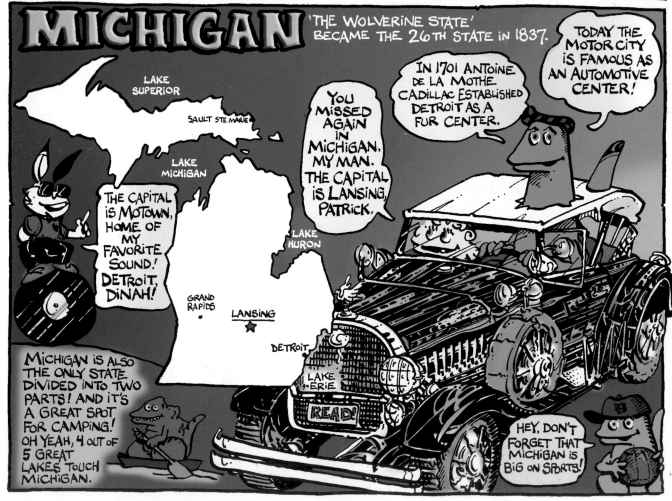

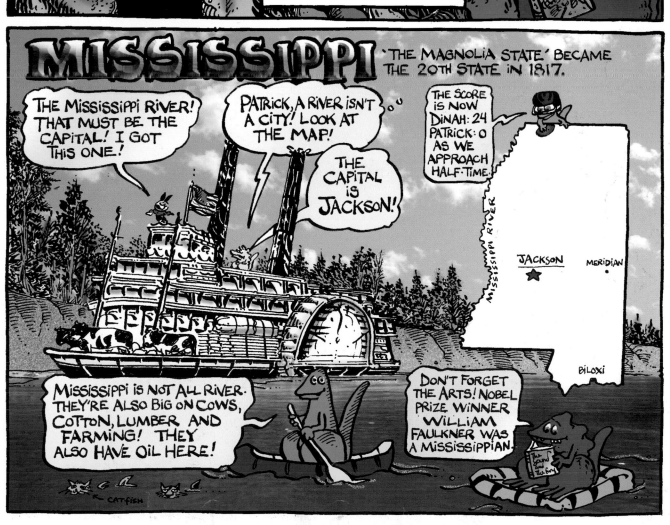

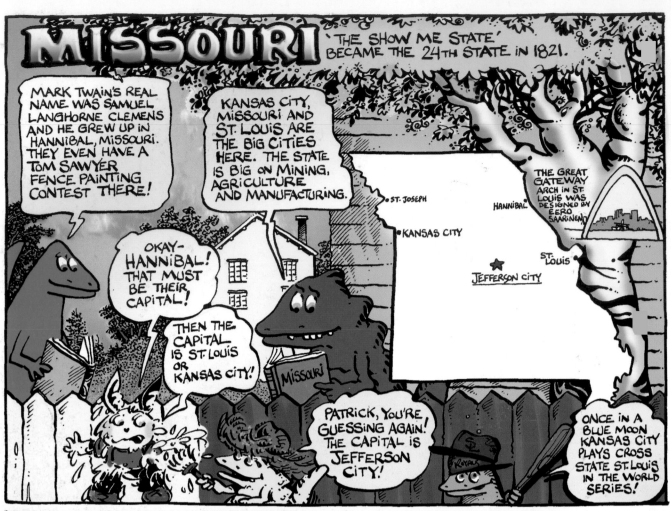

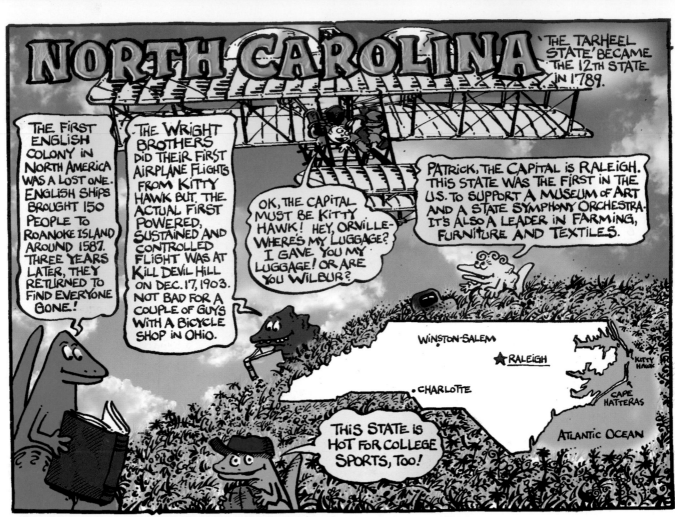

NORTH CAROLINA

'THE TARHEEL STATE' BECAME THE 12TH STATE IN 1789.

THE FIRST ENGLISH COLONY IN NORTH AMERICA WAS A LOST ONE. ENGLISH SHIPS BROUGHT 150 PEOPLE TO ROANOKE ISLAND AROUND 1587. THREE YEARS LATER, THEY RETURNED TO FIND EVERYONE GONE!

THE WRIGHT BROTHERS DID THEIR FIRST AIRPLANE FLIGHTS FROM KITTY HAWK BUT THE ACTUAL FIRST POWERED, SUSTAINED AND CONTROLLED FLIGHT WAS AT KILL DEVIL HILL ON DEC. 17, 1903. NOT BAD FOR A COUPLE OF GUYS WITH A BICYCLE SHOP IN OHIO.

OK, THE CAPITAL MUST BE KITTY HAWK! HEY, ORVILLE- WHERE'S MY LUGGAGE? I GAVE YOU MY LUGGAGE! OR ARE YOU WILBUR?

PATRICK, THE CAPITAL IS RALEIGH. THIS STATE WAS THE FIRST IN THE U.S. TO SUPPORT A MUSEUM OF ART AND A STATE SYMPHONY ORCHESTRA. IT'S ALSO A LEADER IN FARMING, FURNITURE AND TEXTILES.

THIS STATE IS HOT FOR COLLEGE SPORTS, TOO!

WINSTON-SALEM
★ RALEIGH
• CHARLOTTE
KITTY HAWK
CAPE HATTERAS
ATLANTIC OCEAN

NORTH DAKOTA

'THE FLICKERTAIL STATE' BECAME THE 39TH OR 40TH STATE IN 1889.

NORTH DAKOTA DOES NOT HAVE MANY PEOPLE BUT IT DOES HAVE POW-WOWS, RODEOS, FISHING, HORSEBACK RIDING, BOATING, SKIING, HUNTING AND ICE SKATING.

WE DON'T KNOW IF NORTH DAKOTA IS THE 39TH OR THE 40TH STATE BECAUSE PRESIDENT HARRISON DELIBERATELY SHUFFLED THE TWO DAKOTA STATE PROCLAMATIONS IN 1889.

UH OH! I'VE GONE TOO FAR! THE CAPITAL MUST BE FARGO!

BACK UP, PATRICK- THE CAPITAL IS BISMARCK.

THIS IS A BIG STATE!

THERE'S A STATUE OF SACAGAWEA* ON THE CAPITOL GROUNDS IN BISMARK.

GRAND FORKS
BADLANDS
★ BISMARCK
FARGO

* SEE IDAHO

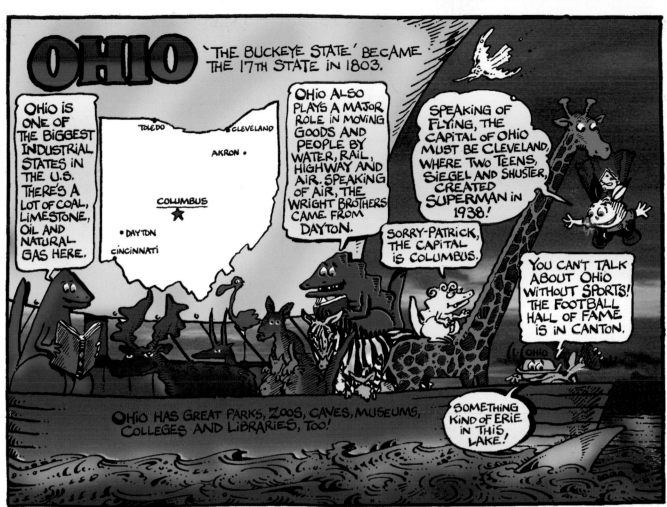

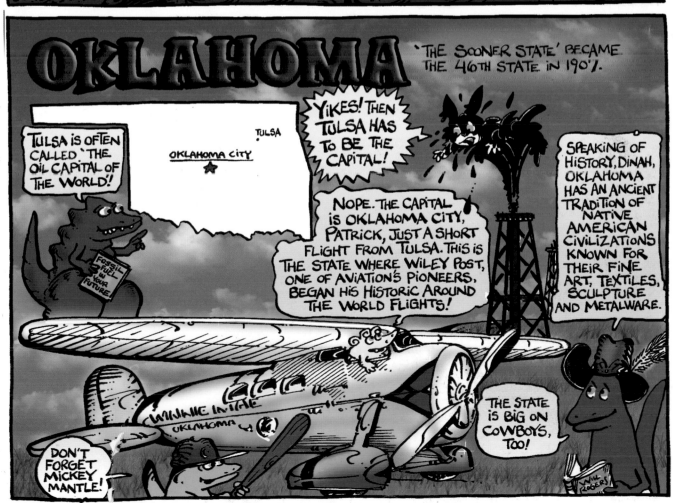

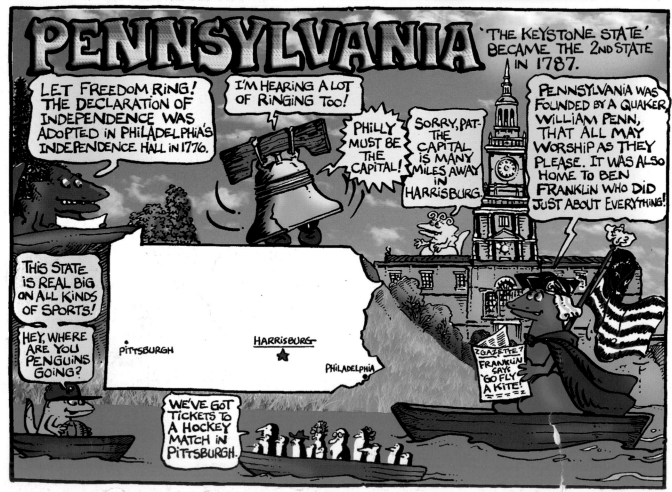

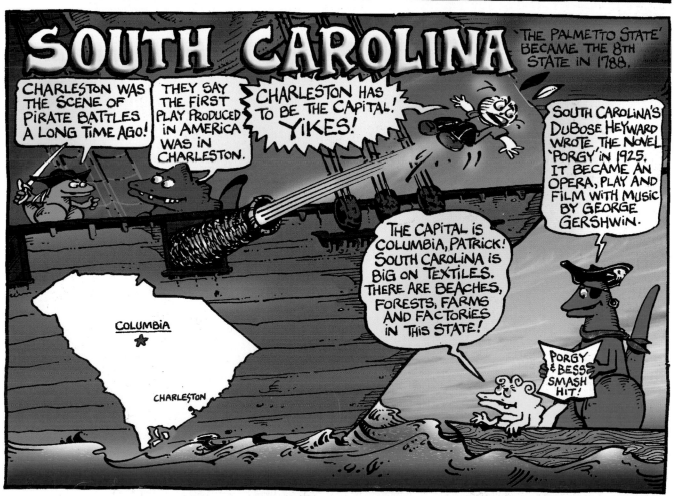

WASHINGTON

'THE EVERGREEN STATE' BECAME THE 42ND STATE IN 1889.

WEST VIRGINIA

'THE MOUNTAIN STATE' BECAME THE 35TH STATE IN 1863.

6/09

dw